I0170026

United Aspects of Satan
The Black Book

Damien Ba'al
John Buer
Penemue

Published by Skeptic, an imprint of HLA Publishing LLC

Copyright © 2016 by Damien Ba'al

All rights reserved. Published in Hell by HLA Publishing LLC

hlapublishing.com

ISBN: 978-0-9968101-9-7

The Baphomet Principle: Self-motivation balanced with compassion and reason, in all things.

Acknowledgements

Special thanks to all the clergy and members of the
United Aspects of Satan

Contents

Introduction

Penemue

In the beginning there was nothing. What a grand way to begin! Nothing says "authority" like starting at the very beginning.

In the beginning there was nothing. Can you imagine it? Of course you can't. For imagination to happen, there has to be an imaginer: you. Which means there is not nothing. There is still you.

In the beginning there was nothing. When you try to imagine it, you conjure up an image of being without distinction. No demarcation lines between "this" and "that", no boundaries between "foreground" and "background", nothing to identify as a thing that can be distinguished from that which is not that thing. It is what you might call "Void".

Only you can't call it "Void". By giving it a name you are creating a category: a distinction, a label. When you assign a name you designate the subject of that name as a named thing, and therefore not nothing. So let's pretend that it has some kind of unpronounceable name, some kind of taboo name. The very first act of creation, then, is your action of creating a category, a name.

In the beginning was the Word. This is the start of your own creation story: not in the historical sense, but in the philosophical sense. How do you create the universe you live in? What are the basic building-blocks of your world view? Choose whatever you like: it's your universe, after all. Your basic building blocks may be atoms or logical axioms, beliefs or goals, relationships or moral priorities. They may be a combination of all of these things. That is your philosophical beginning, a foundation on which you can build the entire structure of your universe.

The United Aspects of Satan is a religion, but it doesn't outline "The Way It Is" with pomp and authority. We start with the idea that everybody builds a unique personal worldview. Your worldview is made up of every aspect of the universe that you live in and experience: from the personal to the social, from moral to metaphysical, from pragmatic to ideological. It is something you create with your assumptions, your experiences, your values, and your will. And like anything you create, you should be constantly working to hone and improve it. This is just as true for your personal philosophy as it is for your professional accomplishments or your relationships. You are the one in charge, and you should never cede control over your worldview to anyone or anything else. Certainly not to a religion.

In the beginning was an Idea. The United Aspects of Satan represents a loose collection of philosophical building-blocks. Some values, some metaphysical axioms, and some basic methods for how to approach life and the world around you. It ties these ideas together with a set of symbols--the personas of the eight demonized gods-- that can help you to apply the philosophy in concrete, real-world situations.

The United Aspects of Satan doesn't have followers. There is a difference between being a follower, and being a traveler who notices when others happen to be walking in the same direction. Satanism isn't a religion you convert to: that implies that you're changing your world-view to fit the needs of the group. Satanism is a religion that you already have inside you. When you read about the building block ideas at the core of the United Aspects of Satan, you may find that you were already walking that same path, even if you didn't use the same symbols or words. You may say to yourself, "That's the philosophy I came up with myself! That is what I already believe!"

How will you know if you're a Satanist?

In the beginning was an Idea. So let's begin....

𝔓urpose and Core 𝔙alues

John Buer

Core Values

The United Aspects of Satan is a religious organization that accepts a metaphorical construct of Satan as a symbolic representation of our values. The values of the United Aspects of Satan are derived from literary and mythological representations of Satan. We reject all depictions of Satan as a being of cruelty and evil, and acknowledge Satan's use by other religions as a scapegoat to maintain the fear of the masses and their obedience to the status quo. Atheistic in nature, we nevertheless define the United Aspects of Satan as a religion, and do not concede the definition of religion to those who believe that religion must contain supernaturalism. Each aspect of Satan that we choose to acknowledge represents one of the core values of our religious philosophy.

Aspects of Satan

Throughout history, mythological narratives and religious traditions have always included a character who represented an adversary or dissenter: one who challenges expectations and rebels against the norms. This character has manifested under different names, and has been imbued with different characteristics depending on the culture that created him. But in a broad historical and literary sense, these characters all can be understood as different aspects of the same underlying character: each with its own narrative, and each symbolizing an important feature of the Satanic worldview:

Satan: Rebellion against arbitrary authority

Ba'al: Perseverance in the face of opposition

Lucifer: Scientific and philosophical skepticism

Baphomet: The use of logic, reason, and empirical evidence to shape our morality

Leviathan: Community for the creative freedom and betterment of every person

Belial: Individualism and individual accomplishment

Pan: Indulgence in the pleasures of life

Loki: The application of humor, fun, wit, and cunning in our endeavors

The Baphomet Principle

Concept by Damien Ba'al and John Buer

Essay by Damien Ba'al

This is a new, small addition to the philosophy. It is separate from The Purpose and Core Values, but acts in conjunction with that. In a way it summarizes The Purpose and Core Values, as well as the moral philosophy in The Narrative of Baphomet. It emerged naturally during the course of a conversation between Damien Ba'al and John Buer.

The Baphomet Principle: Self-motivation balanced with compassion and reason, in all things.

The later part of this, "compassion and reason, in all things" is a major theme of what The Narrative of Baphomet builds to. That is a good reason to invoke the name of Baphomet. Traditionally, balance was the primary meaning behind Baphomet. So you can take this part of it as a balance between the moral and the intellectual, and of feeling and logic.

As shown in The Narrative of Baphomet compassion and reason work when taken together. So they also work as being on one side together. That is where the beginning of the statement comes in. Satanism and The Left-Hand Path have traditionally been about individualism and a motivation and drive that come from within. Rather than emulate a group behavior, one looks within for direction.

This self-motivation is in balance (as one would expect from the symbolism of Baphomet), with compassion and reason. It balances the individual with the community, or balances The Leviathan with Belial. The confidence in oneself and one's knowledge, is balanced with reason, so as not to fall victim to one's own biases. One's self-interest is kept in balance with compassion for others.

This gives us a short statement with multiple layers of meaning that sums up the UAoS philosophy, and provides a good, general guideline, by which one may live.

𝔖𝔞𝔱𝔞𝔫

"Satan literally means adversary. Satan is primarily opposition and rebellion. It is the unbowed will in the face of oppression, the eternal rebel versus the ultimate dictator. It is an unrelenting rebellion waged against the antitheses of Satanic ideals and deeply held beliefs."—Narratives 1(Satan): 1-3

The Narrative of Satan is the first chapter in The Satanic Narratives: A modern Satanic Bible, and introduces the aspect of Satan: representing rebellion against arbitrary authority.

Invoking the name of Satan is inherently a call to action. In mythological literature, Satan is not passive: rather, Satan is always actively working to undermine power structures and deconstruct the assumptions of the powers that be. To be a Satanist, then, is more than individualism and self-identity: it is about the way you relate to the community as a whole.

Ba'al

When you open your eyes, and look around you, you see you are not the only one cast out of society. With the light of reason no longer obscured by a mass collective of the docile and credulous, you can see the arbitrary social conventions, norms, and roles, for the irrational, detrimental things that they are." —Narratives 2(Ba'al): 23-24

The Narrative of Ba'al is the second chapter in The Satanic Narratives: A modern Satanic Bible, and introduces the aspect of Ba'al: representing perseverance in the face of opposition.

Many people ask Satanists: "Why not just say you are atheists? Doesn't it just hurt you to take on the mantle of such a maligned label?"

But a Satanist embraces outsider status. Satanists know that it makes life harder when you are quirky, a rebel, an outcast, a "weirdo", a freak... but the benefits of individuality outweigh the costs. When you accept looks of judgment from others as a compliment rather than an embarrassment, you embrace that aspect of Ba'al.

Lucifer

"[The] requirement for preexisting evidence should be a prerequisite for all knowledge. The philosophical and scientific skeptic believes no objective statement of any significance without reason or empirical evidence. This is the beginning of knowledge and wisdom." —Narratives 3(Lucifer): 32-34

The Narrative of Lucifer is the third chapter in The Satanic Narratives: A modern Satanic Bible, and introduces the aspect of Lucifer: representing scientific and philosophical skepticism.

A Satanist should not just be a seeker of the light of wisdom, but should be a bringer of light, as well. To identify with the Lucifer aspect is to be a teacher, a trainer, a helper, and a coach. As a Satanist, you do not suffer fools and you do not waste your time on those who are not interested in learning; however, you are willing to give of yourself to those who are eager for greater understanding.

Baphomet

"The nature of reality is: Shit Happens. Many events are largely beyond one's control. There is no intentionality guiding anything. We are adrift in a chaotic universe, like a raft with no rudder or paddles, flowing through different currents, winds blowing us in different directions. One can exert a certain amount of influence, and accomplish things, but life is not fair, and a great many things are beyond one's control." —Narratives 4(Baphomet): 18-22

The Narrative of Baphomet is the fourth chapter in The Satanic Narratives: A modern Satanic Bible, and introduces the aspect of Baphomet: representing the use of logic, reason, and empirical evidence to shape our morality.

Rationality means evaluating the world you live in with reason and logic, but rationality is not cold. There are many who make the mistake of thinking that being "rational" means ignoring emotions, or being unfriendly or uncaring. But for a true rational observer, emotions are a very real and very important type of data. Values, feelings, and the connections you have to the ones you love are also very real data, and must therefore rationally be given their due weight in any decision that you make.

The person who fails to take into account xir own feelings, or the feelings of others, is behaving irrationally. The person who tries to pretend that joy and caring are not part of the real outcomes of behavior is ignoring evidence... and going down that path means you are divorced from reality, just as much as you would be if you ignored the evidence of economics, biology, or physics.

The Leviathan

"Through communal emergence, you can create a very a powerful adversary. One that can bend the world, just a little, to the desire of your will. One that can affect change to a greater extent than could any one person. It is the closest thing there is to magic. Its power is limited only by the community and their combined creative energies." —Narratives 5(Leviathan): 25-28

The Narrative of Leviathan is the fifth chapter in The Satanic Narratives: A modern Satanic Bible, and introduces the aspect of Leviathan: representing community for the creative freedom and betterment of every person.

The United Aspects of Satan encourages a balanced approach to the character from which we draw our inspiration: all of the aspects have something to teach us, and all can give us insight. The stereotypical "hermit on the hill" individualist, the "I've got mine and I don't care what happens to you" libertarian, focuses on Belial at the expense of Leviathan. Such a person has narrowed xir worldview and personal growth by ignoring the evidence that we all exist as interconnected social beings. Such a person is not behaving rationally.

The Leviathan, on the other hand, operates under the slogan: We are legion! We are the chaos, the swarm. We understand the difference between being sheep following a leader, and being a collection of individuals who happen to be walking in the same direction, seeing the power that can result.

𝔅elial

"Being an individual, thinking for yourself, and refusing to blindly follow are critically important and definitive traits of Satanism. It should be pointed out that this is different from stubbornness and contrarianism. Being a reverse sheep really is not any better than being a regular sheep." —Narratives 6(Belial): 6-8

The Narrative of Belial is the sixth chapter in The Satanic Narratives: A modern Satanic Bible, and introduces the aspect of Belial: representing individualism and individual accomplishment.

In the early days of Modern Satanism it was fashionable to say "I am the god of my reality!" or that people should "worship themselves" as gods. This kind of dramatic language is fine, for those who need it. It serves a function. If you are breaking free from the oppression of a religion that has taught you that you are nothing unless you grovel at the feet of an invisible spirit, it can be healthy to spend some time recovering from that psychological abuse, and reclaiming your sense of importance and autonomy.

But once that healing has been done, consider this: To be a true individualist, all you need is to love and respect yourself. Love yourself enough to be filled with self-confidence when striving to your goals. Respect yourself enough to follow your own will, regardless of whether it conforms or does not conform to the society around you. Others may see you as being "selfish" or even acting like you think you are a god. But you will know you are embracing the aspect of Belial.

𝔓an

"Pan symbolizes indulgence, hedonism, sex, music, drink, food, celebrations— everything that makes life fun and enjoyable. Traditional religions view all these things as evil. It is the exact opposite for the Satanist. There is nothing to be gained from deprivation."—Narratives 7(Pan): 1-4

The Narrative of Pan is the seventh chapter in The Satanic Narratives: A modern Satanic Bible, and introduces the aspect of Pan: representing indulgence in the pleasures of life.

Satanists appreciate sensual pleasure, worldly experience. Some enjoy sexual deviancy or altered states of consciousness. Many refer to Satanism as a "carnal religion." But the point of sexual deviancy isn't mere rebellion or unhinged debauchery. For a Satanist, seeking out all the pleasures of earthly experience is just a part of your right, as the supreme ruler of your own life, to explore your own lusts and desires in a controlled way. Pan is a connoisseur of earthly experience.

Loki

"You can certainly reach goals regarding very serious things through the use of pranks. People tend to think you are not serious, and underestimate you. This makes your cunning and trickery all the more effective if you need to employ it in order to realize a particular goal." —Narratives 8(Loki): 9-11

The Narrative of Loki is the eighth chapter in The Satanic Narratives: A modern Satanic Bible, and introduces the aspect of Loki: representing the application of humor, fun, wit, and cunning in our endeavors.

Satanists don't mind making mischief and mocking deeply-held beliefs. It goes hand in hand with independent thought and trying to stir up the status quo. We are the jester that speaks truth to power.

We are the fun-house mirror held up to show the absurdity in society. We dare to start conversations that the rest of the world refuses to start.

But do not make the mistake of thinking Satanism is "nothing but" trolling, or that it is all a joke. Our beliefs are sincere and deeply-held belief, made no less so by the fact that we have a sense of humor. Our ability to laugh at any beliefs–even our own–is not a mark of insincerity. It is merely our embodiment of the aspect of Loki: the only god who dared to mock the other gods, and show them up for their absurdity.

Baphomet: The Altered Narrative

Damien Ba'al

*I am quite happy with The Narrative of Baphomet, and will not
be revising it. However, the later part of the narrative can be
explained just as well in a different way. This new way of stating it,
will now be the way the UAoS states it, going forward. It goes along
very nicely with the Purpose and Core Values and The Baphomet
Principle. With these things in place, no endorsements are required.*

*If you go to The Narrative of Baphomet in The Satanic
Narratives, you will notice a paragraph that starts the same as the
first paragraph below. That is when you switch from the published
Narrative of Baphomet to this. I put it together like that in the next
section.*

This brings us to an understanding, where we can have certain moral truths. These truths can be expressed in a code of ethics. You can also express them with greater precision, by simply going over the fundamental concepts that are the pillars of modern secular ethics.

Arguably the most important thing is a pair of concepts that go together. These important ethical concepts are consent and bodily autonomy. Consent, permission, or willingness are subtly different ways of expressing desire and intention.

These concepts are critical in regard to a number of things, but happen to go well with bodily autonomy. One's body and making decisions about that body are fundamental and prerequisite to many other things. One may be unable to provide consent due to illness, being unconscious, age, or cognitive disability. Most of the time people are able to make such a decision and having that choice is fundamental to all ethical concerns.

Being able to decide for yourself varies in importance depending on what it is, with one's body being the most critical. You cannot really have any other freedom without a right to your body and your life. No one can ever violate the body of another without violating an ethical foundation central to the legal code of any modern, civilized society.

This brings us to personal freedom. Maximizing one's personal freedoms should be the goal, and in conjunction with that, one must respect the personal freedoms of another. Taken in conjunction with the first pair, that means no one gets to tell you what to do with your body. It also means you must respect the body of another, and listen to their wishes.

Personal freedoms are not limited to something as basic as people themselves. It also covers speech, religion, and more. One has a right to one's freedoms and an obligation to respect the freedoms of others.

Admitting and correcting mistakes is another basic concept. No one is perfect. Apologies and forgiveness will always be needed. Not every situation where there is conflict is going to call for it, but some of them will. This is a situation where there must be mutual consent.

The final idea is that these basic concepts here, regardless the form or forms they may come in, are always superior to any written code. No legal system of any kind can take precedence over these fundamental concepts.

The raw moral feelings and reason combine to give us these concepts. One can also consider these concepts in the context of one's raw moral feelings, and then apply reason again. In this way, one shapes their ethics and morality.

The Narrative of Baphomet (new)

Damien Ba'al

This is the new version with the material from The Satanic Narratives joined with the essay from the previous section.

Baphomet symbolizes balance, human nature, and the natural world. The human-centric focus of Lucifer works in conjunction with this to give us a robust, naturalist morality, with a proper basis for our normative values.

Balance, in the context of Baphomet, shows us two opposing extreme opposites. The meaning is that these two things are not the only choices—a whole infinity of gray may exist between them, and frequently the two extremes do not exist at all. Good and evil do not really exist in the way they are used as a label on people. Thought and behavior is a mix of these things, too scrambled to isolate a definitive "good" or a definitive "evil".

There is a school of thought that one should turn the other cheek when wronged. Another that says you should not, but instead you should exact vengeance and retribution. This is a false dichotomy. Furthermore, either option is highly illogical and asserts meaning on concepts, which are tenuous at best.

Forgiveness can be a wonderful thing, but exposing oneself to the risk of further negative events is highly irrational. There is no reason why you must follow the other one either. Vengeance and retribution are meaningless concepts invoked by primitive savages, usually in the context of superstition. They solve nothing, and are merely an indulgence in catharsis. There is not anything inherently wrong with this catharsis, but many fool themselves into thinking it accomplishes something other than stroking one's emotions. It is sometimes counter-productive. You may burn a bridge you will need to cross, and your emotional indulgence can work against you if you are not careful.

The nature of reality is: Shit Happens. Many events are largely beyond one's control. There is no intentionality guiding anything. We are adrift in a chaotic universe, like a raft with no rudder or paddles, flowing through different currents, winds blowing us in different directions. One can exert a certain amount of influence, and accomplish things, but life is not fair, and a great many things are beyond one's control.

The universe has no objective moral code, and without that or any gods, there can be no truly objective morality. At this level, nothing matters, and no outcome is better than any other. Morality begins at this place of nihilism and chaos.

We must have some sort of basis for our morality, for the value judgments we make. Many people looked to nature to do this, and that is certainly the right direction, but it is not so simple. The problem with ideas like survival of the fit and strong is it assumes a fairness that simply cannot exist in this chaotic reality. It also ignores the group survival advantage, which is critical to natural selection in any social species such as humans. Finally, it tries to make a value judgment, or assert the way something should be, based only on what is. The existence of something in nature contains no information regarding how that thing should be.

The group survival aspect that is ignored can be made a focal point. This action also solves the other two problems. Understanding that we are a social species, and we evolved to survive as a group, is critically important. Surviving as a group allows us collectively to compensate for negative events that happen in our chaotic reality.

It also gives us something we call a conscience. This is what we call our raw moral feelings. As a social species, we have these feelings in common, as they are a product of our evolution. They are subjective as they are feelings, but because we all have them, we can treat them as if they were objective. It is kind of like every single person liking chocolate ice cream the best. Chocolate would not objectively be the best flavor, as it is a subjective experience, but being universal would mean it could be treated exactly the same as something that is an objective fact.

This is the basis and beginning of morality. We can use logic, reason, and empirical evidence to shape and improve this morality. However, at the same time illogic, superstition, ignorance, and good old-fashioned stupidity can corrupt one's moral compass.

We can also use reason to decide on actions we should take based on these moral feelings. So while it starts with a feeling, it being virtually universal allows it to be treated the same as something objective. Reason and empirical evidence are objective. Therefore, you can have a sense of what is more right, and what is less right. This highlights where on the spectrum something is, as far as how positive or negative its effects would be.

This brings us to an understanding, where we can have certain moral truths. These truths can be expressed in a code of ethics. You can also express them with greater precision, by simply going over the fundamental concepts that are the pillars of modern secular ethics.

Arguably the most important thing is a pair of concepts that go together. These important ethical concepts are consent and bodily autonomy. Consent, permission, or willingness are subtly different ways of expressing desire and intention.

These concepts are critical in regard to a number of things, but happen to go well with bodily autonomy. One's body and making decisions about that body are fundamental and prerequisite to many other things. One may be unable to provide consent due to illness, being unconscious, age, or cognitive disability. Most of the time people are able to make such a decision and having that choice is fundamental to all ethical concerns.

Being able to decide for yourself varies in importance depending on what it is, with one's body being the most critical. You cannot really have any other freedom without a right to your body and your life. No one can ever violate the body of another without violating an ethical foundation central to the legal code of any modern, civilized society.

This brings us to personal freedom. Maximizing one's personal freedoms should be the goal, and in conjunction with that, one must respect the personal freedoms of another. Taken in conjunction with the first pair, that means no one gets to tell you what to do with your body. It also means you must respect the body of another, and listen to their wishes.

Personal freedoms are not limited to something as basic as people themselves. It also covers speech, religion, and more. One has a right to one's freedoms and an obligation to respect the freedoms of others.

Admitting and correcting mistakes is another basic concept. No one is perfect. Apologies and forgiveness will always be needed. Not every situation where there is conflict is going to call for it, but some of them will. This is a situation where there must be mutual consent.

The final idea is that these basic concepts here, regardless the form or forms they may come in, are always superior to any written code. No legal system of any kind can take precedence over these fundamental concepts.

The raw moral feelings and reason combine to give us these concepts. One can also consider these concepts in the context of one's raw moral feelings, and then apply reason again. In this way, one shapes their ethics and morality.

𝔚𝔥𝔞𝔱'𝔰 𝔖𝔞𝔱𝔞𝔫𝔦𝔠 𝔄𝔟𝔬𝔲𝔱 ℜ𝔞𝔫𝔡𝔦𝔞𝔫 𝔒𝔟𝔧𝔢𝔠𝔱𝔦𝔟𝔦𝔰𝔪?

Damien Ba'al

I wrote an essay in the past about the very few characteristics, which define Satanism in all its variations. It is on facebook in various places. This will go into the way some falsely attribute certain ideas as being definitively Satanic, as well as attacking the fallacious logic used in parts of LaVeyan philosophy.

People will commonly say that everything Anton LaVey wrote in The Satanic Bible is definitive of Satanism. Other than false claims that he invented Satanism, this idea essentially boils down to "because LaVey said so in his book". That is not even an argument so much as a lame excuse, and LaVey did not invent Satanism. He just invented modern Satanism, and made it popular.

When I say LaVey invented modern Satanism and popularized it, I mean modern in a colloquial sense, and not in a historical sense. The word modern has a very different meaning in a historical context.

The gods of various defeated tribes were equated with Satan, and many adherents of minority religions were considered Satanists. It was a way to dehumanize and demonize the out-group. To this day, there are still people who worship some variation of these gods.

Theistic Satanists of today are the modern manifestations of traditional Satanism. For theists, what defines Satanism is a simple matter of their belief in some deity or spiritual entity that is equated to Satan. They follow a traditional sort of theology, with the exception of having predominantly Left-Hand Path philosophies.

Things get more complicated with atheistic Satanism as there is no deity of any sort involved. We have to consider what we mean by Satanism in this atheistic sense, to understand what makes something definitively Satanic.

It is universally accepted that Satan means "adversary", or the one who opposes. In the atheistic sense, Satan is a metaphorical construct. It is an archetype defined by this adversarial, oppositional quality. The definitive traits of Satanism are therefore primarily based on these qualities of the archetype. In this way, Satan becomes symbolism for the philosophy consistent with its metaphorical meaning. It provides iconography as well, which also symbolize these philosophical concepts.

Taking the traits of different characters from mythology that have been equated with Satan, is the most legitimate way to construct a Satanic philosophy and religion. That is because it follows the same idea that defined Satanism to begin with. That original idea is of course the adversarial quality of the Satan archetype, which defines Satanism. Therefore, you build on it in exactly the same way. These characteristics from mythology become part of the symbolism, and in the same way as the adversarial quality, they form the basis of a corresponding piece of philosophy. These philosophical concepts can be combined in ways that form a coherent whole.

Regardless the basis in characters from mythology, all parts of the philosophy are subject to reason and empirical evidence. Dogma, tradition, and personal feelings are not an argument. I intend to apply this sort of scrutiny.

Due to the nature of Satanism, one can incorporate any number of things into their personal philosophy. A basis in mythology is the most legitimate way, but there are many ways to craft a variation of Satanism. However, if something has no basis in mythology, considering it definitive of Satanism as a whole, seems quite laughably arbitrary.

We must examine certain "sacred" ideas and see if they have any basis in mythology, and if they can withstand the scrutiny of reason and empirical evidence. Many people go about claiming what is and is not Satanism with annoying pomposity. Ironically, these claims are not based on mythological characteristics, but rather seem to be arbitrary add-ons, and the arguments are full of logical fallacies.

The ideas people falsely equate to being definitive of Satanism have a couple of things in common. The first is that LaVey wrote them in The Satanic Bible. The second is that he got the ideas from sources, which have absolutely nothing to do with Satanism. They all came either from the book, "Might is Right", by Ragnar Redbeard, or from Ayn Rand's philosophy of Objectivism.

If one cannot come up with further justification beyond a particular idea being in The Satanic Bible, then they have no proper argument. This is an argument from authority, and it is dogmatic. Not only is the logic here fallacious, but it is inconsistent with the individualism that is central to Satanism.

There is no greater irony than calling people sheep while going around dogmatically quoting a book. The irony goes off the charts when the statements being made are also logically fallacious.

Consider for a moment how it would be if LaVey was more into reading John Locke. Would different attributes of empiricism then be equated to Satanism instead of Objectivism? What if he was inspired by Rene Descartes? Would Cartesianism be equated with Satanism? What if he was into David Hume, or Bertrand Russell? There is no particular reason why these philosophies have anything to do with Satanism. It is much the same with Objectivism.

The section of The Satanic Bible titled "Love and Hate" is quoted constantly. It is the one that starts off with the following sentence: "Satanism represents kindness to those who deserve it instead of love wasted on ingrates!" People use that entire section to justify things they already think. It is an example of confirmation bias. Some people think that justifies being a total ass to others and precludes helping their fellow humans.

In "Love and Hate" LaVey is quite correct that you cannot love everyone. He logically proves his point. While there are different kinds of love, and you can love everyone in those ways, LaVey meant love in the more conventional sense. You can tell from the context what he meant by the word "love". What he meant by love is something you definitely cannot apply to everyone due to the reasoning he provided.

LaVey also conflates love with kindness in that same section. He proves his point on love and then fallaciously applies that to kindness. He provides no reason why you cannot be kind to everyone though. He just slips it in via the logical fallacy of conflation.

LaVey then proceeds to set up a false dichotomy between his philosophy of selfishness and vengeance, and ideas of loving one's enemies and turning the other cheek. As there are numerous other possibilities without accepting either option, that is a logical fallacy. This false dichotomy is used to equate everyone who opposes his ideas of vengeance and selfishness with advocates of turning the other cheek, loving your enemies, and that sort of thing. This sets up another logical fallacy called a strawman argument. This false argument is then attacked rather than the actual argument.

When the Randian Objectivists in ritual robes go about preaching what true Satanism is and what it is not, they rely on this fallacious logic. Being selfish and being a jerk to people is held up as a virtue, and Satanists who are being kind and helping others are told they are not real Satanists. They quote Love and Hate (argument from authority), which conflates love with kindness (conflation), and establishes the proposition that anyone in disagreement must be adherents of turning the other cheek, loving one's enemies, and that sort of thing (false dichotomy). They then argue against those aforementioned ideas (strawman).

So in order to make the case that going around being a dick is awesome and makes you a super Satany Satanist, and that those being kind to others are just posers and fake Satanists, one must ignore the basis of the ideas, the confirmation bias involved, and employ no less than four logical fallacies. The technical term for that is: Bullshit!

That is not to say that all such folks are advocating being a dick. That is just one example. They can be advocating any sort of selfishness, social Darwinism, vengeance, retribution, or whatever.

If one wants any intelligent, educated person to take them seriously, they must come up with much better than that. Things that are "Satanic" for no other reason than LaVey said so, and amount to nothing more than a contrived attempt at shoehorning the ideas of Rand into "Satanism", will elicit nothing but contempt and derision from any proper intellectual.

If it is to be called Satanism, and arguments are made that it should be applied to every Satanist, it could at least have a basis in mythology, as the name is in regard to this archetype out of mythology. In my variation, I make no claim that it should apply to Satanism in total, but rather only to my specific variation. I still base all the characteristics on the traits of these Satan-like characters from mythology. Every bit of my philosophy corresponds to that in some way. That is the proper basis for a religion and philosophy you name after such a metaphorical construct.

Regardless where you get the philosophy, it must survive the scrutiny of reason and empirical evidence. I wrote mine with that idea in mind. However, the most quoted bits of LaVeyan philosophy do not survive such scrutiny as I have shown. Arguments made from that contain at least four logical fallacies. That is utterly laughable. I cannot take such an argument seriously at all.

I am not even going to get into the Social Darwinism. That has been replaced by new scientific research, which LaVeyans are apparently not aware of. Internet access and five minutes should be all you need to debunk social Darwinism. There is plenty of research about group selection, and the evolution of various social species.

With all this in mind, I hope to hear less arrogant declarations about who is and is not a real Satanist—or which things are Satanic and which things are not. It is utter nonsense, and it comes from people who demonstrably have no proper argument at all.

The Path

Damien Ba'al

In a previous essay I explained how the idea that Satanism must be selfish comes from LaVey incorporating the philosophies of Ayn Rand into his variation. The basic idea, however, is neutral. It is just the rebellion and opposition to arbitrary authority of the adversarial archetype, as well as the individualism of the Left-Hand Path that are definitive. Everything else is just part of a variation.

Some people have said that the Left-Hand Path is selfish because it is focused on the self. That is given as the reason why Satanism is selfish regardless of whether or not one accepts Randian Objectivism. It is stated, that at the very least, those who are not selfish are on the Right-Hand Path, rather than the Left-Hand Path.

This is a misconception. The external may or may not indicate which path one is one.

It is the Right-Hand Path that is concerned with the external. The Left-Hand Path is neutral on that. Therefore, one cannot easily determine the path of another—at least not without understanding the motivations in question. The Left-Hand Path looks within. It is about understanding the self, and being directed by one's own will. The Right-Hand Path is about surrendering one's will to something external, and then joining with that. In this way, one would be directed from without, rather than from within.

It is all about the desire of the will. If one is directed from there, without blindly accepted external influence, then one is on the Left-Hand Path. Whether one is a famous philanthropist, or the most selfish jerk the world has ever known, it matters not. It is about one's will alone directing the individual to be one or the other of those extremes. Likewise, if one is influenced from without, so as to conform to the ideal of another or others, then one is on the Right-Hand Path. Once again, it is irrelevant whether this motivates one to be generous or selfish. Only the source of the motivation matters.

If one is being selfish solely because they think a Satanist, or one on the Left-Hand Path must do this, then one is not truly on the Left-Hand Path. The individual in this example is surrendering the will to the external ideal. It is only Left-Hand Path if one is selfish from the motivation one's own will. The same thing goes for the charitable individual. What is the source of the motivation? What directs the individual in question?

This may sound like some sort of new-age thing. That is because new-age nonsense is cobbled together from ideas lifted from eastern religions. Eastern religions are mostly Left-Hand Path. I can assure you that there is no mystical bullshit involved here. It is just that the mainstream, western, exposure to the Left-Hand Path comes from all that hippie humbug. To understand this, one must forget the past associations, and let Left-Hand Path philosophy stand on its own.

The Left-Hand Path is about looking within, and letting the force of one's will, motivate one's actions. That is just one thing though. It is also about the discovery of self. Getting to know yourself, who you are, and what you are about, is an important part. Another part is acceptance. You must accept who and what you are, or work to change that.

Change brings up the topic of self-improvement and personal accomplishment. Improving the self and driving oneself to achievement are the Left-Hand Path way of life. One must always continue becoming a better person, and achieving what one wills.

Fulfillment of the self is another major part of this. This has to do with what one desires. It can be mental or physical. It only matter that it is of the self. It can involve external actions, but does not have to. It only matters that this is directed from within.

The question has to do with reasoning. Why is one selfish? Why is one generous to others? Doing what is directed from the will within, makes it Left-Hand Path. Conforming to what one thinks their path must be, is Right-Hand Path.

In conclusion, bringing one's path into this is just as irrelevant as invoking Satanism itself. Selfishness is not definitive. It is optional. It depends on what is within, which in turn determines whether or not one is drawn to the Rand-inspired elements of Satanism codified by Anton LaVey, or the more egalitarian elements codified by Damien Ba'al. Individualism and the adversarial archetype are the elements they both have in common.

Associations and Terminology

Damien Ba'al

So the "non-theist" thing is going on again. It has an ebb and flow. It's the same as "atheist", meaning everyone outside the criteria of theist (I say everyone as the ist suffix is the personal form of the word). They are just taking a Greek root word with the Greek prefix meaning 'everything other than the root word', and changing it to the Latin prefix meaning the exact same thing. It's the same thing as referring to plants that use reproductive methods other than sexual, as non-sexual instead of asexual.

While some people try to say there is a difference in meaning, usually people admit that it is just because "atheist" has certain associations and a cultural identity, and non-theist doesn't as it was a fairly recently coined term.

One group that has been using this is American Humanists. I can kind of see their point. It's still pandering because they are saying they are non-theist, while at the same time including people who identify as atheists in that, just because some take issue with the associations of the word "atheist".

I find it silly, but if I was in charge of American Humanists, I'd be on the fence. They can use "non-theist" so as to avoid having to discuss the distinction from certain kinds of atheists. When identifying as atheist, one has to contend with associations of the fedora-wearing neckbeard who spews hate at any and all religious people. So I can see their point.

With The Satanic Temple, who is the other prominent group using the term "non-theist", I don't get it at all. It's a very different situation than with the American Humanists, although the reasoning is the same. A few might try act like the meaning is different, but generally it's about the cultural identity and not contending with those associations.

TST spends a lot of time on the term "Satanist" though. They do identify with that, as a Satanic organization, and defend the use of the term. So they have articles at length addressing the associations of "Satanist" from various sources. There are the really nasty Satanic

Panic associations about child/animal sacrifice, and that conspiracy theory stuff. Then there are associations with theistic Satanism, including actual theistic organizations. Then there is the Church of Satan, and all those associations. These are deeply ingrained, and many people have quite a reaction to any word with "Satan" as part of it.

They can do all of that stuff, with Herculean effort, countering the most awful associations. But then they don't want to address the associations of "atheist", and demonstrate the difference between them and fedora-wearing neckbeards who troll people on the internet and write xenophobic rants about Muslims. Honestly, the entire argument of "we aren't the neckbeard atheists" is contained within the "we aren't LaVeyan Satanists" argument. Highlight the appropriate section, CTRL-C, go to new post, CTRL-V, done.

For the way I run things, I just stick to the proper terminology. No fucks given about associations, and no desire to pander to those whose entire issue with a word, is things they read into it, which have nothing to do with the meaning. This is 10x as true for an organization with "Satan" in the title, such as mine, for example.

I'm an atheist, meaning that I am not a theist. Theist is a person with a belief in some sort of deity. I don't have that. "Atheist" means I'm outside of that. It doesn't say how far outside of that though. Just like "non-apple" applies as well to orange as to aardvark, so it is with "atheist". I'm also an agnostic, meaning that I don't think most concepts of gods are even knowable or falsifiable. I also find so many different, major philosophical problems with these concepts, that I consider them to be nothing but meaningless fabrications.

It also says nothing of my wider views of materialism and skepticism. So gods are a silly idea, with no meaning beyond the actions of the large number of people who live under such false assumptions. Every philosophical proposition is treated in the same way, as is every empirical claim. So I end up an atheist because of a rational position on the issue of belief regarding one little idea, due to handling it the same as the seemingly countless other ideas with any sort of objective component.

The "Ba'alean Satanism" of the United Aspect of Satan is a massive collection of various philosophies, which is typical of Satanism. The differences are how you combine things together. I don't run from labels or the associations of others. I'm interested in associating only with people who critically examine any given thing, and I have no desire to convince those who presuppose associations for which they have no basis. Ignorance maintained in spite of collecting knowledge is antithetical to everything I do. I also don't tell anyone what to think. Individuals must decide if my ideas resonate with them or not, and more importantly, know what they think and why.

Satanic Household Chores

Penemue

In my household, we have a very Satanic way of dividing up the domestic work. If I'm bothered by the number of dirty dishes in the sink, I wash them. If I don't have the energy to wash them, I don't. But I don't ask my partner to wash them either. If xe is bothered, xe will wash them. If not, the dishes don't get washed... until they build up to the point where someone has both the energy and inclination to do it. Then it gets done.

Usually I wash the dishes, because my threshold for "being bothered" is much lower. But it's my choice. Nobody tells me that it's "my chore", and I never resent being the one who does it because, ultimately, I do it because I want the dishes to be clean: that is my own desire.

By contrast, I never mop the floor. I probably will never mop the floor, because I find it boring and messy and aggravating. My partner finds it relaxing, so xe mops the floor. This is how we divide up all of the tasks: not by edict, not by assignment, not by command or imposition of will of one person on the other. Whichever person minds doing the chore less, or wants it done more, ends up doing it. The result is what scientists call a "self-organizing system."

I say that this is a very Satanic method for dividing up the chores, because it reflects multiple values of the United Aspects of Satan. Neither one of us is putting demands on the other. Neither one of us is bargaining or holding the other person hostage. Each of us is reflecting the aspect of Belial by performing the tasks we want done the most, at the time that we want it done. We are reflecting the aspect of Satan by refusing to let conservative traditional cultural and religious proscriptions tell us which partner is "supposed" to carry out what task. And we are reflecting the aspect of The Leviathan by understanding that we are working together, even as we individually pursue our own priorities: I know that xe dislikes cleaning the toilets more than I do, so I take on that task… and let xir mop the floors instead. I am mindful of how my actions impact the entire household, without begrudging or placing demands upon anyone else's independence.

You might think it silly to use something as mundane as household chores as a way to expound on Satanic morality; but really, what is the point of morality if you can't apply it to the day-to-day operation of your life? That is what life is, after all, minute by minute and day by day, the million little choices that you make.

I also think household chores are a good illustration of Satanic morality, because many people have a misconception that Satanism is a kind of lone-wolf, beating-your-chest individualism. This is a leftover from the outdated "Might Makes Right" attitude in the original "Satanic Bible" by Anton LeVay (I'm tempted to refer to it as "the Old Testament of Satanism"). But for the United Aspects of Satan, individualism is strengthened by community, just as every community is strengthened by the independence of its individuals.

And what better way to illustrate that then to think about a household, and the way you manage day to day tedious chores with the ones you love? The relationships that are the healthiest allow for both mindfulness of how each person affects the other, as well as individualism and independence of all of the people involved.

Many people don't realize it, but that dynamic — individual mutualism, coordination without the imposition of will — is deeply Satanic.

Ave Satanas.

𝔓𝔰𝔶𝔠𝔥𝔬𝔱𝔥𝔢𝔯𝔞𝔭𝔶 𝔦𝔫 𝔱𝔥𝔢 𝔇𝔢𝔰𝔢𝔯𝔱

Penemue

Fame and faith can consume a man. They can make for a deadly combination. Imagine the man who had so much of both that people became convinced that he was divine… and he allowed himself to be convinced, as well. If you saw him walking through the desert, muddled with hunger and delusion, your heart would surely go out to him. You would want to help. Of course you would.

When I was in college, a friend of mine suffered from a psychotic break. He was eventually diagnosed with acute schizophrenia, but that diagnosis only happened later: after he'd stopped eating, shaved his head declaring that he didn't have the "right" to own hair, and then tried to poison himself. I saw him in the hospital that night, his mouth ringed with black from the charcoal the medics had force-fed him, his eyes red and wild. And it threw me back to all the conversations I'd had with him in the months leading up, where I could tell that something was wrong but I didn't know what.

He was an intelligent guy, and very articulate. But he would phase in and out of lucidness, his mind wandering off into conspiracies about "higher powers" and creatures that were always watching and who would punish you if you made bad decisions. Sometimes he would claim he had powers himself, and that the rest of the humans were "mere shadows" compared to him.

Those conversations were frightening, because he was so plainly earnest. He believed to the core of his being, every word that he said. So, I tried to use the only conversational tactics at my disposal: logic and reason. I asked him for evidence. I challenged his logic. But nothing I could say would penetrate his delusion. "They are watching us," he would simply mutter over and over again, "they see everything."

When I imagine Lucifer in the desert, watching over a rail-thin man who has been starving himself for weeks on end, my heart goes out to that poor fallen angel. Lucifer is seeing a man who is wrecked by mental illness, a man who is on a literal path to self-destruction. The man is consumed by the myths and stories that people tell about him, and that he believes about himself.

If I were in Lucifer's shoes, I'd want to help poor Yeshua, too. Lucifer knows the importance of evidence and skepticism, so naturally he tries to use that tactic to get through to Yeshua:

"If you are really some kind of divine being, then why don't you throw yourself off of this cliff? Come on, if you really believe all this stuff: prove it with your actions rather than your words!"

But it couldn't break through the mental illness of Yeshua's faith, who simply replied: I don't need to provide evidence, I know what I know.

It reminds me of my schizophrenic friend in college: coherent, semi-rational, but completely unable to recognize the delusion in his own thoughts.

After Lucifer gave up on Yeshua, Pan decided to give it a try. Pan knows the importance of earthly pleasures and indulgences, and his heart went out to the starving man in his self-imposed abstinence. "Hey, bro... at least make yourself come bread and eat. What are you accomplishing by starving yourself?"

But Yeshua's mental illness consumed him, and he claimed that he didn't need actual food, he could survive just on his own willpower and beliefs.

Finally, Satan appeared, and attempted to reason with Yeshua one last time: "You're destroying yourself in abasement to some imaginary being who has imaginary rules… this is absurd! Why are you doing this to yourself? Bowing down to an invisible, impalpable, unknowable entity is insane, don't you see that? You might just as well bow down to a rock! Or a horse! Or, even me! That's how ridiculous it is!"

Quite naturally, when this story was transcribed by others, they described these events somewhat differently. But this is how it actually happened.

And you should think about how you would act, too. What would you do, if your friend was out there, a shattered man, broken by mental illness, killing himself in the desert with paranoid delusions about superpowers and an invisible being watching over his every move. How would you try to help him?

Would you try to reason with him, like Lucifer?

Would you try to get him to take care of his body, like Pan?

Would you try to get him to see the oppressiveness of his delusion, like Satan?

Maybe you would take a different tactic completely. But if you have any compassion in you at all, you would surely do just as the

Devil did, 2000 years ago on Mount Quarantania, when he tried to talk poor Yeshua out of his delusions and bring him back to the eternal light of reason.

ℑolitical Correctness ℑs the ℑevil

Penemue

People like to keep things simple. Whenever possible, they would prefer to have One Big Problem, rather many different ones.

The Devil is a perfect illustration of this principle. Over hundreds and thousands of years, mythic and historical writing has included a number of bad characters harboring ill will, or representing challenges to humanity. But our simple-minded culture has decided that they are all actually just one Super-Bad Being: the Devil.

In the Book of Job 1-2, Job has a spiritual adversary who is referred to as "the satan" (which translates from the Hebrew as "the adversary"). According to the book of Job, this being is specifically

Job's adversary: not "the adversary of God" or "the adversary of mankind". The satan is in fact following God's instructions, according to the story. And yet, in our modern-day interpretation of the myth, this being becomes "The Devil".

In Leviticus 7:17, the Hebrew word sair is translated as "The Devil", even though it really means "goat" or "satyr".

In Deuteronomy 32:17 and Psalms 106:37, the Hebrew word shed is translated as "The Devil", even though it means "idol".

In 1 Kings, the word "satan" is used to refer to an actual human being: Rezon of Damascus. He was an adversary (a "satan") to Israel. But many Christians claim this passage refers to The Devil.

"Shaitan" or "ash-Shayṭān" is also the name of Iblis in Islamic myths: the one who whispers evil temptations into the ears of man. According to many: also the Devil.

A snake in a garden that tempts Eve? Must have been the devil.

The peacock angel worshiped by the Yazidis? Must have been the devil.

And my favorite bit of twisted interpretation is Ezekiel 28:12-14, which many, many Biblical scholars argue must be referring to the Devil:

"Thus says the Lord GOD: You were the signet of perfection, full of wisdom and perfect in beauty. You were in Eden, the garden of God; every precious stone was your covering, carnelian, chrysolite, and moonstone, beryl, onyx, and jasper, sapphire, turquoise, and emerald; and worked in gold were your settings and your engravings…"

And so on, and so on. The passage goes on to say that he was proud because of his beauty, and so the Lord cast him out. Many Biblical scholars call this a description of the Devil.

The only problem with this description of "The Devil" is the one sentence that precedes it:

"Moreover the word of the LORD came to me: Mortal, raise a lamentation over the king of Tyre, and say to him……."

This (supposedly inerrant?) biblical passage very clearly states that it is a description of the king of Tyre, not the Devil. But no! It's too confusing to have more than one Bad Guy in the novel of life… so Christians claim that this, too, is a description of The Devil.

This over-simplification happens in other areas of life, too. A good example is the way that America's right-wing has chosen to focus on "political correctness" as the supposed source of so many things it finds disagreeable.

The original idea behind political correctness was fairly mundane: be mindful about how the things you say might have unintended negative consequences or might impact people around you in negative ways.

But now?

Students are complaining about their classes? It's because of political correctness!

President Obama won't use the phrase "Islamic Terrorism"? Political correctness!

Women are being allowed in the military? Oh, the horrors of political correctness!

Conservatives want to make "political correctness" synonymous with "language policing" and authoritarianism. And admittedly, some radical "PC Police" activists can use the term in a very authoritarian way. As a Satanist, and a strong supporter of Loki, I'm against anyone who tells me that I should never offend people, or must walk on eggshells in the way I talk.

But it is also obvious to me that political correctness has become the American Right's modern "Devil": the single big Bad Guy that can be blamed for all of the problems!

Well, you know what? I like the Devil. And I also like political correctness: at least in the way it was originally intended, even if not the way it is executed by some on the left-side fringe. It is noble, and indeed very Satanic, to be mindful of one's place in a culture, and one's relationship to other people. It is very Satanic to be aware of the power you have with your own rhetoric, and as an activist within a community. It is the very nature of the aspect of The Leviathan.

So let the political right wing wrings its hands over the devastation being brought down on the land by the dreaded Political Correctness! As a Satanist I say:

Hail Community. Hail Political Correctness. Hail Satan.

The Balancing Act

John Buer

The fourth Core Value, "The use of logic, reason, and empirical evidence to shape our morality," is derived from the Aspect of Baphomet. Those who are familiar with Eliphas Levi's famous illustration of Baphomet will recognize the creature as a symbol of balance–human and animal, male and female, dark and light, to name a few things that Baphomet represents. Baphomet is also a symbol of reason, a representation of the weighing (or balancing) of evidence in order to perceive one's circumstances correctly and therefore make choices in accordance with right thinking.

For the theist who acts in accordance with "God's will," right action is not determined by reason but by blindly following the dictates of deity. We as Satanists cannot afford to make this mistake, nor do we act in a contrarian manner towards what ideas are presented in holy books simply for the sake of being contrarian. There are some who identify as Satanists who think and behave in this manner, but they are simply being contrarian. Satanists do not choose to do the reverse of theists in an effort to be "evil," they decide to act based on reason and not the marching orders of God.

When a supernatural deity is out of the picture, the Satanist is then accountable to himself or herself. He or she must not only take personal responsibility for his or her actions, but he or she must also act in a way that is true to himself or herself. Knowing oneself is key to determining right action. One must behave honestly and consistently with his or her values. He or she must possess the self-disciple necessary to constantly re-evaluate his or her actions through introspection.

If a wrong is committed against the self, he or she should resolve to amend his or her actions. If a wrong is committed against another, he or she should reach out to the other person and try to correct the wrong. Being accountable to oneself means taking responsibility for one's actions, not blaming one's faults on external factors, especially not a supernatural source.

To the Christian, forgiveness is given freely and immediately, for even the most egregious of offenses. To the Satanist, forgiveness, even the forgiving of oneself, is something that usually has to be earned. What is earned holds value, and we value right action that is balanced by reason and self-knowledge.

Hail Baphomet! Hail Satan!

Darkness and the Void

John Buer

The attraction that many Satanists have towards the darker side of life is often misunderstood. Far from being a form of mere attention-seeking or a symptom of depression, the cultivation of a dark aesthetic can be empowering.

The awareness of one's own mortality can motivate the individual to have a greater appreciation for life.

The acknowledgement of the chaotic and merciless nature of the universe can wipe away the delusions of specialness that leave one ill-prepared to cope with misfortune once it strikes.

The recognition that there is no meaning to one's own existence beyond what he or she chooses to make of his or her life is sobering, but also fuel for the fires of ambition.

The understanding that there is no God to save us places the responsibility that we have towards ourselves and our fellow human beings squarely upon the shoulders of each of us.

From the Void comes a hunger for pleasure, a source of perseverance and strength, the desire to achieve something of personal significance, and compassion and empathy for one's fellow human beings, for each of us is subject to the whims of chance.

To peer into the Abyss long enough that the Abyss peers back into you is to experience the strength and sense of purpose that the darkness brings. Let it flow through you like a river. Let it burn like a flame inside your heart. Call upon it when you reach out for the warmth of your lover. Feel its presence when you must overcome whatever challenge you face.

For within the Void lies unbridled passion.

The neophyte will learn this with time and, hopefully, with mentoring. His or her projection of a dark aesthetic is a fledgling attempt to harness the power that he or she desires. This should not be treated with ridicule, but understanding. Those with experience should guide the neophyte back to the Void, and help him or her to know the reason why he or she seeks power in the first place. Help the neophyte recognize how vulnerable he or she is to an uncaring universe, and then show him or her that the understanding of that vulnerability is the source of wisdom and strength.

May your days be filled with passion, and may you achieve all that you desire.

Hail darkness! Hail Satan!

Carpe Diem Carpe Semper

John Buer

Today I would like to share some advice related to the aspects of Lucifer and Pan as they represent the search for self-knowledge and pleasure. The attainment of both of these goals is related to an understanding of the self, which can reveal personal barriers to deeper levels of knowledge and enjoyment. While experiences that produce knowledge and enjoyment lead to personal growth, one can, without being aware of what he or she is doing, limit the effect of his or her growth by not being attentive to possibilities for even greater development.

There is always more, until you stop searching for it. To assume a boundary to what you can learn from an experience, or to not bother to further examine what an experience can teach you, is to place limitations upon your personal development. The hardest chains to break are the ones that you make for yourself. You may have some freedom to move within those chains, but you will not go as far as your potential would allow.

For example, consider the experience of first falling in love with another person. The experience is exhilarating, to open yourself up to another person and allow them to see your vulnerabilities as well as your strengths. But this is also an opportunity for further development, to find very specific nuances of the experience that can lead to greater self-awareness. What is it about the other's skin that makes you long to touch him or her? What does the other's vocal inflections and speech patterns reveal about his or her personality, and what makes that interesting to you? Does the other person have a quirk or a tic that you find attractive, and do these behaviors reveal anything to you about the way that you see yourself?

There is always more information to learn about the experience as long as you can find another question to ask yourself. So probe for more information about your experiences as fully as you can, and soon you will discover that it becomes even easier to analyze an experience and draw even more information from it.

My addition to the old Latin proverb, "Carpe diem," or "Seize the day," would be this: Seize the day and keep seizing. Do not allow the potential for grasping more information about yourself and your experiences to pass you by. Living life to the fullest means continually expanding your concept of the limitation for where "the fullest" can be.

Hail experience! Hail Satan!

The Myth of the Myth of the Satanic Community

John Buer

The idea of a Satanic community is only a "myth" to those who lack emotional intelligence and common sense. Those Satanists who can rise above their elitist myopia long enough to make nice and gain the friendship of others are truly masters of one of life's most important skills: not being a fucking douchebag.

In fact, so many possibilities open up for the non-douchebags of the world–personal, professional, and romantic possibilities–that a self-aware person would puzzle over what anyone could ever hope to gain from acting like a snobby little shit in the first place.

As we Satanists search for the best ideas, separating the wheat from the chaff, let us spare the misanthropic malcontents among us none of the ridicule that they rightfully deserve. For in their devaluation of others, they also devalue themselves, leaving themselves only to hold up hollow accomplishments as "proof" of their supposed superiority. What they lack in their ability to touch others' hearts and minds, they try make up for with... stuff. They trade the ability to inspire for the ability to acquire, and they are all the poorer for doing so.

A wise person knows that the ability to see value in others, and to help others increase their value, will inevitably benefit him or her to a greater extent than his or her singular efforts ever could. There is a difference between self-interest and selfishness, though a fool will always conflate the two. One who is motivated by self-interest would naturally not want to be treated like an asshole, and one of the best ways to accomplish that feat is to not act like one, to not hold oneself in such high esteem that he or she cannot be surprised by or learn something new from other people of any walk of life.

Some have posited that Satanists would not get along with one another in a community setting, because of each Satanist's fierce individuality. However, individuality is not a factor in how well one can get along with others. The ability to get along with others is determined by one's level of maturity and his or her emotional intelligence. Humility, the asset that an immature person views as a liability, also plays a major factor in gaining likability. Maturity, emotional intelligence, and humility are not exclusive to fierce individuality.

Those who hail snobbery as a virtue are a truly sad lot, but worse are the people who allow themselves to be devalued to such a point that they would want to gain the snobs' approval. Though an "elitist" might say that he or she is only maintaining some kind of standard against mediocrity, the individual who does not feel beholden to the arbitrary standards of others is the one who maintains his or her worth. That person never spends a night secretly hoping that he or she has kissed the requisite amount of ass to be considered one of the cool kids.

This is not to say that Satanists should not have standards for the other people that they interact with. We have no respect for foolishness. But it would be wise to hold maturity and likability in higher esteem than one's ability to have a lot of stuff, or project his or her superiority onto others.

𝔐𝔶 𝔉𝔞𝔳𝔬𝔯𝔦𝔱𝔢 𝔖𝔞𝔱𝔞𝔫𝔦𝔠 𝔥𝔬𝔩𝔦𝔡𝔞𝔶

John Buer

The idea of a Satanic holiday is almost absurd to me. I say "almost," because I celebrate a lot of holidays, but in the back of my mind, I am always a little bothered by the meaning of the word itself: holy day. As I reject all that is holy, surely I should reject the idea of a holy day, and yet I recognize the purpose of choosing certain days of the year to celebrate certain occasions.

One does not have to believe in the supernatural to respect the idea that marking certain days special is a way to celebrate the turn of the seasons, the sacrifices of those who have come before us, and the promise of a new year. Holidays are occasions that represent different aspects of life, both joyous and tragic, and reflecting upon their meanings can give us a greater appreciation for ourselves and our place within the grand scheme of existence.

There is one holiday that I cherish above all others, because it is a Satanic holiday, if you will pardon the apparent oxymoron. As I equate Satanism with living a joyous, fulfilling, and purpose-driven life, this particular holiday best captures the essence of those ideals. It is a day of standing tall with a heart that swells with pride in oneself and one's accomplishments. It is a day of bearing down against the obstacles that stand in one's path, and declaring, "I shall not be overcome!" It is a day to laugh, to cry, to be vulnerable, to be strong, to experience both joys and heartaches. Most importantly, it is a day to make the most of oneself and one's circumstances.

My favorite Satanic holiday is called Today.

How will you spend your Today? Will you be a victim, or will you be victorious? Will you establish a new connection with others, or deepen an existing relationship? Will you create something that will last beyond this day, or beyond all of your days? Will you allow fear to prevent you from new experiences, or will you indulge, with all of your heart and mind, in all of the pleasures that Today has in store for you?

I challenge you to celebrate Today with all of your being, no matter what happens. Don't squander this most precious of holidays. Do that which will bring you in greater alignment with your values and your goals, and remove every unnecessary or harmful element from your path. For this Today may be the only one you have left, so spend it wisely, but courageously. Go forth with strength and grace.

Hail Today! Hail Satan!

®n the Pretense of Power

John Buer

The universe is not an ATM for wishes. It has no interest in manifesting your desires, no matter how often you pretend to project your psychic beams of hopefulness into it.

The path of the Adversary should not lead you to the same delusions as the faithful. You exist in a universe that is entirely indifferent to your being, except for those times when the universe is merciless. To experience reality as it truly exists, you must cast aside any notions of intercession by benevolent forces.

If it hasn't happened already, you will one day find yourself in a situation that cannot readily be wished away. What good will your illusions of occult power be then? Better to get rid of your illusions now, before you realize only too late that what you thought was magic was mere confirmation bias and placebo.

I will trade all of the imaginary power in the world to walk in the Luciferian light of truth. I will see my existence as it truly is, my strengths and weaknesses exposed and undeniable. Only then may I act in a way that will cause me to have an effect on my circumstances.

The Adversary is the enemy of falsehoods, even falsehoods that bring comfort and pleasure. Do not settle for the pretense of power, when goal-setting and goal-striving can bring to you the real thing. Let the believers live in their world of shadows, while the shadows flee before the light of Lucifer.

May the light of Lucifer shine upon us all. Hail Satan!

How to Make a Deal with the Devil

John Buer

Once you become an outspoken Satanist, it is amazing how many people will approach you and ask how they can make deals with the Devil. When it happens to me, I usually tell them, "You can't make a deal with the Devil, because the Devil doesn't exist." Then I explain to them that as an atheistic Satanist, I see the Devil as a metaphorical construct that represents my values, not a deity to be worshiped or a demon with whom to make pacts.

It usually goes right over their heads, which is fine: once their infatuation with the Devil is over, I expect them to try to make deals with someone or something else. The greatest trick that superstition ever pulled was in convincing the world that there are shortcuts to growth and self-empowerment.

Those who are familiar with some of my other writings know that in the place of magic, I practice something I like to call "persistent effort towards a well-defined goal." This is not to say that I do not engage in ritual, because the act of devising my goals and writing them down on paper is, itself, a ritual. Neither do I really have to write them down, I suppose, as long as I have decided what they are, but actually seeing the words written down on paper is satisfying to me, because it makes my thoughts appear to be more "concrete" or "real."

However, there are no occult forces in play. The words I create are just words until I put forth the effort to bring my desires into reality. There is no connection between my intentions and the greater universe. Things Above are not connected to those below, except by coincidence or wishful thinking.

To those who define magic as "changes in consciousness," I shall say that doing practically anything causes changes in consciousness, but unless you put yourself in a state of consciousness that actually motivates you to do something, changing your consciousness isn't a particularly useful or special act. The one thing you won't find in a book of the occult is the notion that everything you do after you've made up your mind, rather than the process you follow in order to make up your mind, is what has the power to create change.

Your Will is the information that travels through your nervous system and results in the un-assing of your seat. It is not a thing that you should childishly enshrine as some kind of special being. I can imagine the number of disgruntled Satanic Witches and Warlocks who are attempting to angrily shoot their beams of Will at me for making such a statement, and I can say that I am experiencing a change of consciousness as a result of that idea: I am becoming amused.

My variation of Satanism has no place for magic and superstition, for I view skepticism and reason as the definitive traits of the Aspect of Lucifer. I know this outlook will likely be disappointing to those who aspire to unlock special, spooky powers of the occult, but if it's any consolation, I have some really great news:

You are going to die. One day, you will stop breathing, your heart will stop pumping blood, and you will die. I mean deader than dogshit, too. You're going to be dead as fuck.

If that doesn't give you a surge of empowerment, then you really haven't yet come to terms with your own mortality. I encourage you to do so, because once you internalize the fact that your time is limited, you will want to spend less of it muttering nonsense by candlelight, with the hopes of causing changes to your consciousness.

If you want to make a deal with the Devil, this is the deal that I suggest you make: To learn, to aspire, to seize the day, and to let nothing stop you, not even yourself. Dispense with self-deceit and foolishness. There is no power greater than the combination of knowledge and effort.

Hail Satan!

True Satanism

John Buer

I've heard enough about "real" and "true" Satanism lately that I've decided to share my thoughts on the matter. I find it somewhat amusing that, among different branches of a religious philosophy that claims to promote individuality and freedom of thought, there is so much passion for the establishment of an orthodoxy to which all members must fervently follow.

When considering the lingering effects of the Satanic Panic and the public's general fear and distrust of all things Satanic, I can understand why many Satanists would want to promote some kind of standard to show that Satanists aren't out to sacrifice everyone's pets and cannibalize their children. It also makes sense that, when someone does something horrible in the name of Satan, other Satanists would want to distance themselves from the person and his or her behavior.

I can also understand those who, as a reaction to efforts to make Satanism more "palatable" to the masses, feel as though the baby is being thrown out with the bath water. There are good conversations to have about drawing the distinction between not being a serial-raping baby cannibal yet not being a sappy little goody-two-shoes.

Too bad the True Satanists out there aren't having any of those conversations.

I'm talking about the Satanists who feel the need to call out others for being "pretentious," then lock themselves away in their ritual chambers and presume to affect the universe with their magical powers. I'm not going to say that these people aren't Satanists, thus avoiding the No True Scotsman fallacy, but I will say that for these people to call themselves "real" or "true" is a bit of a stretch, as their esoteric meanderings denote a distinct detachment from reality and truth. As I believe that my variation of Satanism helps me to deal with the real world as it truly exists, not as I would like to pretend that it is during my Harry Potter cosplay sessions, I feel like I at least practice a variation that is more real and true than theirs.

"True Satanist" is a title. How funny that those who seek to claim it are usually the first ones to decry the descriptive and functional titles of other Satanic organizations. If you're going to claim that someone hasn't "earned" a title yet call yourself a "True Satanist," it would at least make sense for you to be somewhat interested in truth, reason, skepticism, and the elimination of, rather than the proliferation of, woo and bullshit.

Hail Truth! Hail Satan!

The Sickening Belief in Divine Intervention

Penemue

"I had a student in my class," she said, "whose father worked in the World Trade Center. And on September 11th, when the school made the announcement about what happened, all of the kids were in shock. But she just started crying and crying. And we spent all day trying to call and find out about her daddy, but of course we couldn't get through."

The woman, a now retired school teacher, was telling this story to a small group of us this afternoon. We had been discussing tragedies, and our memories of where we were during great events in history.

"Now, her father had worked there for 30 years, and had never missed a day of work in his life. But the day before, on Monday September 10th, he had been feeling really sick, and he picked up some Nyquil on the way home from work. He took it that night. He wasn't even planning on taking the next day off of work. But he took the Nyquil, and he slept through the alarm, right into the afternoon. He had never missed a day of work in his life, but he missed that day. He had no idea what had happened. We finally got in touch with him at 5:30 pm. He was still at home, feeling sick. He had no idea what had happened."

"That's just amazing," a man replied.

"Can you imagine? He'd never been out sick, never even taken a vacation, but on that day….." she said, letting her voice trail off wistfully.

"Well, I'll tell you: that's divine intervention, right there!" the man announced.

I said nothing.

…but this is what I thought:

HOLY SHIT YOU ENORMOUS ASSHOLE!

Are you saying God chose to intervene in the natural course of human history in this specific moment, and "saved" exactly 1 man while allowing almost 3000 other people to die?

Are you saying that every single one of those 3000 were less deserving of life than this girl's father? That the feelings of loss of the young daughters and sons of the 3000 others did not matter enough to warrant God bending the normal natural rules of time and space... But only the feelings of this one girl did?

Everyone has xir own definition of "god", and while I roll my eyes at all of them, some of them are at least palatable. The "blind watchmaker" God who sets the universe in motion at the beginning of time and then refuses to intervene, for example, is a weird contrivance for whom there is no evidence... but at least he's not an asshole.

The God that this man believes in is a cruel disgusting sociopath who makes a point of reaching into his creation to save a single life while destroying thousands of others. For absolutely no reason.

I didn't say anything, but I was thinking: The fact that you would choose to believe in such a God is perverted. By raising one person's good fortune onto some kind of pedestal you are telling the entire rest of the world: Fuck you. In that moment, you weren't important enough. God was there for someone; God was not there for you.

So when you see a Satanist who seems angry about religion, or angry about God, remember this story. I can't speak for all Satanists, of course. And not all Satanists are angry. But if you're ever asking yourself, "Gosh, why is it that some Satanists seem so filled with hatred towards God?" just remember this story.

If a Satanist expresses hatred for someone's perception of God, there is a good chance it is because that person's God is hateful.

For The Love of Satan

John Buer

My love is intense and all-consuming, raging like a fire that
burns in the heart of hell. It is a declaration of my existence and the
manner in which I choose to exert my emotional force upon the
universe. My love is a reflection of my values and the motivating
force behind many of my endeavors, for as I love others, so do I seek
to grow and acquire for the sake of love.

It is a misconception that the Satanist is a hateful person,
incapable of loving others. As many theists declare that "God is
love," they assume that whoever would take the path of the
Adversary must naturally be against love. But God is not love; God
is imaginary. Love is an emotion that one can experience

independently of a belief in God. The Satanist stands in defiance to the idea that a prescribed set of theistic beliefs should inform the way he or she chooses to love.

The Satanist is guided by the Luciferian light of reason in all matters, including the way in which he or she chooses to love. This is why it is acceptable for the Satanist to have romantic love for an adult person of the same gender, but not romantic love for a child, as children are not developmentally mature enough to handle relationships with adults. Apparently the Church is confused on both of these matters, following the ways of God and leaning not unto their own understanding, as they do.

As Satanists challenge religious and societal norms, so would they challenge the notion that reason alone is not sufficient to determine who they should love or how they should love others. Love is not a thing to be reserved only for those who conform to the status quo, but a feeling that can be shared with those who are not beholden to the arbitrary rules of the masses. Thus Satanic love increases the value of those who embrace outsider status, instead of allowing them to be deemed unworthy because of how "different" they might be.

This is not to say that Satanists do not have standards for whom they love, but those standards are not arbitrary rules dictated to them by God and society. A Satanist is first and foremost the adversary of self-denial and blind obedience. The love of a Satanist is as fierce and unbridled as the Satanist himself or herself.

Hail Love! Hail Satan!

But What Is It All for, Damien?

Damien Ba'al

You see Atheistic Satanism, these local autonomous communities, and the United Aspects of Satan, but wonder what it is all about. With the exception of myself, no connection can be ascertained from a mere cursory examination. One must dig deeper, or alternatively, listen to my explanation.

People are rightly wary when they hear of new organizations. Self-serving cults spring up all over, all the time. The nasty C word has been hurled at me a few times. With an "L", not an "N", silly. All right, yes, that one too, but you know what I mean.

Things like critical thinking, individualism, skepticism, and self-leadership are at the very core of my teachings. Mindless automatons blindly marching in my footsteps are neither desired nor tolerated. Such people are sought out by the unethical and narcissistic, to stroke the ego and stuff the wallet.

I prefer individualists who happen to have converging goals and interests. There is no following on this Left-Hand Path. One simply walks along, as one desires, but looks around and notices those who happen to be on the same path. Rather than anyone following, or going out of their way, they all simply go where they will, communing with their neighbors along the way.

With the things I teach, I would be the worst cult leader ever, as would any proper Satanist. The cult of critical thinking, seems much like the submarine with screen doors or the solar powered flashlight.

Atheistic Satanism is an entity named after a category of religion. This centralized organization consists of a website, a social network, and a facebook page and group. It's more generic, and draws a wider audience. Rather than an echo chamber, it seeks to compare similar, but distinctly different points of view.

This generic nature facilitates sharing and exploring different views from various individuals. It seeks a harmonious balance of compatible similarity and contrasting heterogeneity.

The UAoS (United Aspects of Satan), is a specific religious organization. It is based on the foundational text, "The Satanic

Narratives: A Modern Satanic Bible". The religion, philosophy, and worldview detailed within that book is represented by the UAoS.

Being that the UAoS represents my specific point of view, it exists only online, as one centralized unit. There may be temporary logical divisions that are fluid, dynamically forming based on activity. However, it is a single organization with no geographically restricted chapters.

This is of course in contrast to Atheistic Satanism, which is much more generic in nature. This lack of specificity allows for the creation of autonomous communities. These communities or chapters are able to operate as separate organizations. The community organizers, or chapter leaders are vetted to make sure they are sufficiently compatible in viewpoint and outlook. Once this is done, there is virtually no oversight on my part. The organizer is granted authority to operate the community as an independent organization.

They are united under the centralized entity as represented by its online presence, for the purpose of finding other Satanists in the same area. The organizers also form a group, which allows for support, the sharing of ideas, and additional purposes as needed.

So they have the centralized support, and the name recognition, but without giving up the autonomy of the community. This gets around the pitfalls of chapters and grottoes. Without the problematic qualities of central authority, hegemony, and hierarchy, the communities are able to thrive.

These autonomous communities, with their innovative solution to the long standing problems of such groups, are then able to act in ways which are meaningful to each individual community. There is a local focus, and it's completely customizable. For what works in one city, may not work in another. The concerns of each community may be as different as the cultures and geological features of the different areas. Yet at the same time, they are not without support.

All of these can be combined to form a complete and fully functional implementation of Satanism. One can also take what one wants, and leave the rest. With complexity, comes additional features, functionality, and customization. So it not only avoids the problems usually inherent in such things, but does so contextualized in the individualism at the core of a Satanist.

With this knowledge, you now know what it is, and what it is all for—but only from the perspective of objective reality. Your customizations allow you to have something truly unique from the perspective of your individual subjective experience. Therefore one must look within to comprehend this in its totality.

Final Thoughts

Damien Ba'al

As a relatively new organization, the UAoS continues to evolve. We prefer it to be flexible in focus and ideas. Philosophy and culture are the general areas of which we are most focused, and where new ideas are being added. As you can see, the philosophy I created as a foundation, has been built upon by John and Penemue, giving further depth, and expanding it with their creative energies.

The Satanic Narratives is the foundation of the UAoS, and the contents of this book should provide a good feel for where we are going with it. There are additional writings on the websites as well. We'll continue to post new content there, and more books will be published in the future.

I'm truly grateful for everyone who has expressed to me, the meaning they derive from The Satanic Narratives. I love hearing from everyone who contacts me, to express the positive impact my writing has had on their lives. I greatly appreciate all of you and the sharing of your experiences.

Hail Satan! Hail to you all!

Links

http://atheisticsatanism.com

http://uaofsatan.org

http://damienbaal.com

On Sale Now:

The Satanic Narratives:
A Modern Satanic Bible

Available in print and E format,

wherever books are sold.

www.ingramcontent.com/pod-product-compliance
Lightning Source LLC
Chambersburg PA
CBHW071600040426
42452CB00008B/1244

* 9 7 8 0 9 9 6 8 1 0 1 9 7 *